copy righted Material

This book belongs to

I'M A
NURSE
whats your
superpower?

STAY SAFE
STAY ALIVE

WORLD'S BEST
NURSE

Wife
Mom
Nurse

NURSES
DO IT
BETTER

NURSE
EVERYDAY SUPERHERO

www.ingramcontent.com/pod-product-compliance
Lightning Source LLC
Chambersburg PA
CBHW081533220526
45467CB00010B/3169